Keeping Mum

A Monologue from *Visiting Hour*

Richard Harris

SAMUEL FRENCH

FOUNDED 1830

SAMUELFRENCH-LONDON.CO.UK
SAMUELFRENCH.COM

ISBN 978-0-573-13291-9

www.samuelfrench-london.co.uk

www.samuelfrench.com

FOR AMATEUR PRODUCTION ENQUIRIES

UNITED KINGDOM AND WORLD
EXCLUDING NORTH AMERICA
plays@SamuelFrench-London.co.uk
020 7255 4302/01

Each title is subject to availability from Samuel French,

depending upon country of performance.

KEEPING MUM

(from *Visiting Hour**)

This monologue, taken from the play *Visiting Hour*, was first presented as a National Theatre Platform performance in the Cottesloe Theatre on 30th September, 1987, with the following cast:

Pauline	Diane Bull
Old Woman	Marcia Warren

Directed by Michael Gambon
Designed by Soraya Walton
Produced by Amanda Saunders

A revised version of the play was presented at the Duke's Head Theatre on 26th June, 1990, with the following cast:

Pauline	Susan Jameson
Old Woman	Angela Rooks

Directed by David Gillies
Produced by Sally Campbell

*Published separately by Samuel French Ltd

CHARACTERS

Old Woman (non-speaking)
Pauline

Plays by Richard Harris
published by Samuel French Ltd

One Act:
Albert
Is It Something I Said?

Full Length:
The Business of Murder
Local Affairs
The Maintenance Man
Outside Edge
Partners
Stepping Out
Visiting Hour

Written with Leslie Darbon:
Two and Two Make Sex
Who Goes Bare?

KEEPING MUM

A hospital ward

A hospital bed with the usual bedside cabinet, visitor's chair, temperature chart and with a set of radio headphones and oxygen outlet above the bed

When the CURTAIN *rises, the ward is in half-light. The bed contains the motionless body of an old woman. She lies on her side, away from us, so that all we see of her is her grey hair. But she should be so small and still that we scarcely notice that she is there*

The Lights increase on the bed area and we hear the distorted jangle of hospital sounds: tannoy messages for doctors, ambulance sirens, patients calling for attention, etc. The hospital noises fade and a handbell rings

After a moment, Pauline enters. She is drawn, neat, fastidious. It is raining outside and she wears a raincoat. She pauses in the doorway to shake out an umbrella. She moves in and stands for a moment, looking at the motionless old woman as though uncertain. She props the umbrella up against the bedside cabinet and puts down her large bag. She moves closer to the old woman, cranking herself up for the ordeal

Pauline (*bending low; quietly but cheerfully*) Hello dear, how are you feeling? Feeling a bit better, are you? You certainly look a bit brighter, there's some colour in your cheeks. And they've done your hair, haven't they, it looks so much nicer, really pretty. (*She is gently touching the old woman's hair*) Who did it for you, the little Irish one?

The old woman raises an arm, murmuring soundlessly. Pauline takes the hand in both of hers and leans close, gently stroking the old woman's hand during the following

What's that, dear? No, it's Friday, today's Friday. Mm? No, you mustn't worry about that, every day's the same when you're stuck in a silly old bed, aren't they? Yes. That's right, you close your eyes and I'll just sit here for a few minutes and keep you company, mm?

She continues to stroke the old woman's hand for a moment, then lowers it gently and moves to sit in the chair

Sorry I'm a bit late, the buses were all over the place. I left at twenty-five past, would you believe. They're always unreliable on a Friday so I thought: right, I'll allow myself another twenty minutes, that should be ample. Nothing like it. I said to him, quite politely, why are you so late, what's the excuse this time? The look on his face, you'd have thought I'd asked him the secret of the universe. In Swahili. We've got two drivers off sick, he said. I didn't pursue it. The truth is, of course, it's raining and we all know what that means, don't we? Two or three drops and they're loath to leave the depot, public transport my eye.

Slight pause

God knows when I'll get the car back. I phoned the insurance people this morning. It's in the pipeline, they said. It's been in the pipeline for over a month, I said, why don't you consult Dyno-Rod? That's what I should have said, anyway. They're quick enough about asking for the premium but when it comes to paying out ... I was quite lost without that car for the first week or two. I'd forgotten what buses were all about. And the fares. I don't know how people do it, I really don't. Dennis is absolutely right. We take far too much for granted. You don't know how lucky you are, he says. I do now. Anyway. Here I am.

It has all come quickly but now the flow dries up. This moment. She looks round at the cabinet. During the following, she gets up to tidy the top of the cabinet, putting tissues, the used paper cup and straw, etc., into the wastebag which hangs inside the cabinet door. All for something to do

Look at this, they haven't cleared your cup away. Oh dear, you haven't touched it again. You must drink, you know, plenty of fluids they said, you must drink plenty of fluids. (*Confidentially*) You know what I think it is — I think it's those straws they give you. You don't like those straws, do you, that's what it is, you're not a baby, are you, you can manage, of course you can. Let's see what we can do when the trolley comes round, shall we? Nasty old straws, who wants to drink out of a nasty old straw, eh? Course you don't. Anyway. Let's have a bit of a tidy up, shall we, get rid of some of this nasty old rubbish. You'll be needing some more tissues by the look of it, I'll have a word with Nurse. Oh dear, look at this, someone's left the top off your water — when did they last change it, can you remember?

She covers the top of the jug with a tissue

There now, that's better, isn't it, we can see where we are now, can't we?

She sits, not facing the bed, more out front. She flicks imaginary pieces of fluff from her clothing: small, birdlike movements. A moment

It's nice and quiet this afternoon. Last week it was like Paddington Station. I expect they get their busy periods like everyone else. I don't suppose the nurses are complaining. Dennis says they like to have a clear out at weekends so that all these doctors can go off yachting or whatever it is they do. Still. Good luck to them, they work hard enough.

A moment

Were you in this cubicle when you first came in, I can't remember, isn't that awful? I had it on my mind all last night, God knows why, but I was trying to picture which cubicle you were in at the beginning and, do you know, I couldn't for the life of me remember. I know the bed was round the other way and they moved it because of the radiator but ... All last night, couldn't get it out of my mind. In the end I had to put the radio on really loud and do a great pile of ironing. Mind you, it needed it, it's been piling up for weeks. I just haven't felt like doing it, there didn't seem any ...

Who's on today, I wonder. There was no-one in the office. The telephone was ringing away and no-one was taking a blind bit of notice. I nearly answered it myself. Well, it's not very nice, is it, phoning up to find out how someone is and not even getting a reply. It doesn't exactly fill you with confidence. People worry, it's only natural. Look at that time I phoned intensive care. After the operation. You go home and get some rest, Mrs Marley, they said — if anything happens we'll let you know. If not you can phone first thing in the morning. What happens? I telephone and I can't even get a reply from the switchboard. I was nearly out of my mind. I've got to go to that hospital, I said, anything might have happened. For God's sake, Pauline, he said, if anything's happened they would have phoned. I don't care about that, I said, I want to go now — now!

Her hands have tightened into fists as she has been re-living her anxiety. A moment

Poor Dennis. It's been so hard for him. He's had the both of us to worry about. I can say it now, and I mean it, but there have been times when I've been terrible to him, said some terrible things. You see, when someone's been ill as long as you have ... I mean, it's not your fault, but ... I just took it out on him, I suppose. Oh well. It's all settled now, it's all ... sorted itself out.

A moment. She realizes she has been twisting the wedding ring on her finger

I popped in downstairs on the way in. Into intensive care. I like to say hello, they were so nice. They still have a good laugh about that night, you know. Talk about strong as an ox, Mrs Marley — we've never seen anything like it, will-power isn't in it. I said, she's always been strong-willed, my mother. I suppose she had to be really, with someone like Daddy for a husband, all that money trouble and gambling and everything. Strange how he took to gambling. He'd gamble on anything. It's a disease like anything else, I suppose.

A moment. From somewhere, the distant sound of a telephone ringing

Tea trolley should be here soon. I wonder if I can persuade her to give me a cup, I'm parched, I really am. I could have some of yours, I suppose, but it's not really fair to mess up their charts. Sister said to me: we really have to be very accurate about the amount of fluid she's taking otherwise it's a complete waste of time.

She was quite short with me actually. Mind you, she looked tired, very tired. And I think she's having problems with her son. I heard her talking to the little Polish one. I'm beginning to sound like a right little busybody, aren't I? Oh dear. You can't help hearing things when you've been sitting around in corridors like I have for the past — what is it — eleven weeks. Eleven weeks, my God. Three months ago I didn't know this place existed and now I could find my way here with my eyes closed. And sometimes I do, sometimes I feel I'm on automatic. Dennis says, for God's sake give it a rest, she'll understand, I mean, good God, it's not as if she even knows you're there half the time ... I said to him, I'm all she's got, she expects it ... and you would, wouldn't you, you've always expected me to ...

That's how I crashed the car, I suppose. I was so tired, doing everything by numbers. They said: we think she's going, Mrs Marley, we think perhaps you should come in. Thank God it was two o' clock in the morning and only me involved. I should have let him drive me in. He just lost patience, I suppose. I can't blame him. And not a scratch on me. I wish I could say the same for the rotten car.

First thing you said when you came out of the anaesthetic: where is she, you said. They couldn't believe it, half an hour after a major operation and you were demanding attention ... she should be out for hours, they said, but there you were, eyes open, fighting to stay awake, forty-eight hours without sleep, they couldn't believe it, will of iron.

And what you called that poor doctor is nobody's business. I'm so sorry, Doctor, I said ... Never you mind, Mrs Marley, he said, it's the anaesthetic, she's hallucinating and you should hear what some of them call me. There he is, trying to save your life and all he gets for his trouble is get away from me, you ugly, black bastard. A mouthful of tubes and still you can spit it out like you've always managed to spit it out. I demand to see the manager, you said, and he'd better not be a blackie like the rest of them. You thought you were in some foreign hotel. Bermuda, I think you said. Only why you should think of Bermuda, I've no idea. You've never been there and, as far as I know, never expressed the desire. Until then, of course. I suppose it must have been all those potted plants and dark faces.

They were so kind to you. We don't take any notice, they said. Besides, she's such a lovely old lady. I felt ashamed.

A moment. Then she looks towards the bed and reaches out to touch the hand resting on the cover

Your hands look nice. They look really nice since you've been in here. Someone's been doing your nails by the look of it. Like a young girl's. So soft and white.

She gently lets go of the hand and looks down at her own hands, turning away from the bed

That's what David said ... I never realized what nice hands Gran has got, they're really nice, a really nice shape. He would have come to see you more often but it upset him so much, he's always hated hospitals. I remember that time I went in for my scrape. I had to say to him: for goodness sake, David. Thanks, Mum, he said, hope you feel better, and he was out of that room quicker than if I'd asked him to do the washing up.

I really enjoyed those four days in hospital. (*Smiling at the thought*) All that lovely rest. I should have been in for at least the week but that was the time you had your heart attack. Suspected heart attack, they were never really sure, were they? Anyway, there I was, on the run again.

You've always been very ... unfortunate in your timing, haven't you? Even on my wedding day you managed to get that terrible migraine and I remember when I was in the school play ...

She gets up suddenly, angrily, and moves forward two or three paces and looks up and down the corridor, giving herself time to calm

Trolley's late. You can hear it coming a mile away. It's got a life of its own, that trolley. Uncontrollable. I watched her the other day, careering down the corridor, ricochetting from one bed across to the other as though she was expecting them to light up, as though it was her personal pinball machine. Perhaps it is, perhaps it's her way of getting back.

She sits. A moment

I just wish more than anything I could get a good night's sleep. I take those pills the doctor gave me, but, I don't know, I drop off and half an hour later I'm wide-awake again. My brain just won't ... shut down. I could take more, I suppose, but I don't want to become dependent on them, I've seen what they can do.

Do you know, never a night goes by without I see Daddy. I mean I go to bed and I close my eyes and I see his face. It's been the same ever since he died, not like when he was ill, not like what he'd become, but as I remember him when I was about, oh, fifteen, I suppose.

I can't remember you as you were. I try, I try to force a picture into my mind but all I ever see is you as you are now. I know what you were like, I remember so clearly, I mean I can talk about it, make a picture out of words ... but inside my head ...

You should have died. They should have let you die, I mean, what was the point? It's spread everywhere, they said, there's nothing we can do except ease the pain, two months, perhaps more, it's difficult to say at her age, sometimes they hang on. Does she know what it is, I said ... No? Then for God's sake don't tell her, she's terrified of death, she always has been, that's why she can't stand being on her own. If she asks, we'll tell her, they said ... if she doesn't ask, it's up to you. But you didn't ask. And I didn't tell you. Just day after day of coming here and pretending everything was going to be all right and going home and what could they give *me* for *my* pain?

I saw that fat woman on the way in. The one with the corset, the one that caused all that fuss, she's back in for a check-up, they'll be pleased. D' you remember how she refused to take her clothes off? I am not taking my clothes off and that is final, she said. She did make me laugh, that sister: if you've got something I've never seen, Mrs Whatever-Your-Name-Is, I'll shoot it. We did laugh. If you've got something I've never seen, I'll shoot it.

She laughs and takes her handkerchief from her bag. A moment

He's gone. Dennis. He's left me. Four days ago. Don't go to that hospital, he said, I want to talk to you. What about, I said — I already had my coat on. Just sit down, he said. I need to talk to you. Don't be silly, I said, you know I've got to go, you know she expects it. He didn't argue. He just said ... yes, that's right, you go to the hospital. When I got back there was a suitcase in the hall and he was sitting in the kitchen with his coat on — what's this, I said, what's happening? He said: I can't stand it any more, that's what's happening, Pauline ... I've done my best, for months I've done my best ... but I can't stand it any more, you need help and I can't give it to you.

A moment

When I say he's left me, I'm not saying it's permanent, I'm saying ...

A moment

You couldn't stay on your own, there was no way you could look after yourself — we agreed. I talked about putting you into one of those homes but he knew I didn't really mean it. You'd never forgive yourself, you can't put her into one of those places, he said, have you seen them? I did have a look at one or two. I just wanted to cry. She's your mother, he said, we'll look after her. If it gets too bad, all right, then we'll have to think of something else.

Four months you were with us. Four months with the smell of death in every room. It was the ups and downs that made it so hard ... One minute sitting up all night, waiting for you to die, the next minute running up and down those stairs, you ringing that bell he fixed up ... where's my drink, where's that sandwich you promised me, you're no daughter of mine, you don't care about me ... I could cope with it when I thought you were going but to see you sitting up in that bed demanding this, demanding that, looking at me like I was a skivvy ... God, how I wanted you to die.

It was me who sent for the ambulance that night, me couldn't cope any more. He said we've had her this long, you'll never forgive yourself if she dies in that hospital, but you didn't know where you were any more ... you were in a coma, all those drugs they kept giving you, all those injections ... I just couldn't face what I had to do anymore ... I couldn't face seeing those sores all over your poor body ... I couldn't face changing one more sheet ... I'm phoning for the ambulance I said, it's the right thing, I know it is. They were there in ten minutes. Only young boys, really. They were so gentle with you.

You looked so ... tiny. Like an empty ...

They didn't think you'd last the night. But even then you wouldn't give in, hour after hour I sat there, day after day, night after night, just looking at you. I went home that night — you were very low, they let me stay 'til, oh, it must have been two in the morning. I'd been in the house ten minutes and the phone rang. We're very sorry, Mrs Marley. I must have said my goodbyes to you a hundred times but when I should have been there ... half an hour I'd been gone. We're very sorry, they said. I came straight back to see you — he tried to stop me but ... I had to see you. You'd struggled so hard and then ... just slipped away. She didn't wake up, they said, it was very peaceful, the best way really. Are you sure, I said. Are you sure she didn't ...

She breaks down and recovers and wipes her eyes with the handkerchief

I didn't cry at the funeral. It didn't seem to have anything to do with
me ... or you ... or anything, really.

A moment

Next day, I brought a big tin of coffee into the nurses — they'd been
so very kind and it was the least I could do to say thank you. They were
very pleased. Then, on the Friday I think it was, I was out shopping and
I saw the bus pulling up at the stop and ... Anyway. I can't expect him
to understand, it's what you have to do, isn't it? But you understand,
don't you, you know why I'm here ... you've always ... I wanted to say
I love you, you know that, don't you? Mum ... I wanted to say it.

*She cries. The old woman stirs in the bed, raising a feeble arm. Pauline
recovers quickly and gets up and moves to lean over the old woman,
taking the hand in her two hands*

Hello dear, how are you feeling? It's me, Mrs Marley, I was just
passing and I know you don't get many visitors so I thought I'd just
pop in and see how you were. Mmmm? Mrs Marley. My mother was
in the next bed — you used to have those little chats. Mmmm? That's
right, yes, I came yesterday. Close your eyes and I'll just sit here for
a few minutes and keep you company 'til the trolley comes round, eh?

*She gently lowers the hand and sits, looking out front again. During the
following, the Lights slowly fade to Black-out*

I would have been here earlier but the buses were all over the place.
I left at twenty-past five, would you believe. They've always been
unreliable on a Friday so I thought: right I'll allow myself another
twenty minutes, that should be ample ...

Curtain

FURNITURE AND PROPERTY LIST

On stage: Hospital bed and bedding. *Above it*: set of radio headphones and oxygen outlet
Bedside cabinet. *On it*: paper mug and straw, jug of water, box of tissues, used tissues. *Inside cabinet*: paper bag hanging on door
Chair

Personal: **Pauline**: wedding ring on finger, wet umbrella, large bag containing handkerchief

LIGHTING PLOT

Property fittings required: nil.

Interior. The same scene throughout

To open: General half-light

Cue 1   When ready
Increase lighting on bed area　　　　　　　　　　　(Page 1)

Cue 2   **Pauline**: "...'til the trolley comes round, eh?"
Slow fade to black-out　　　　　　　　　　　　(Page 10)

EFFECTS PLOT

Cue 1   To open   (Page 1)
*Distorted jangle of hospital sounds: tannoy messages,
ambulance sirens, patients calling for attention etc;
fade after a while; handbell rings*

Cue 2   **Pauline**: "...like anything else, I suppose."   (Page 4)
Distant telephone ringing

PRINTED IN GREAT BRITAIN BY
THE KINGFISHER PRESS, LONDON NW10 6UG